A Note to Parents

DK READERS is a compelling program for beginning readers, designed in conjunction with leading literacy experts, including Dr. Linda Gambrell, Professor of Education at Clemson University. I   National Reading Co   and the College Reading Association, and has recently been elected to serve as President of the International Reading Association.

Beautiful illustrations and superb full-color photographs combine with engaging, easy-to-read stories to offer a fresh approach to each subject in the series. Each DK READER is guaranteed to capture a child's interest while developing his or her reading skills, general knowledge, and love of reading.

The five levels of DK READERS are aimed at different reading abilities, enabling you to choose the books that are exactly right for your child:

Pre-level 1: Learning to read
Level 1: Beginning to read
Level 2: Beginning to read alone
Level 3: Reading alone
Level 4: Proficient readers

The "normal" age at which a child begins to read can be anywhere from three to eight years old. Adult participation through the lower levels is very helpful for providing encouragement, discussing storylines, and sounding out unfamiliar words.

No matter which level you select, you can be sure that you are helping your child learn to read, then read to learn!

LONDON, NEW YORK, MUNICH,
MELBOURNE, AND DELHI

Series Editor Deborah Lock
Designer Sara Nunan
U.S. Editor John Searcy
Managing Art Editor Rachael Foster
Production Georgina Hayworth
DTP Designer Ben Hung
Jacket Designer Mary Sandberg

Reading Consultant
Linda Gambrell, Ph.D.

First American Edition, 2007
07 08 09 10 11 10 9 8 7 6 5 4 3 2 1
Published in the United States by DK Publishing
375 Hudson Street, New York, New York 10014

DK books are available at special discounts when purchased in bulk
for sales promotions, premiums, fund-raising, or educational use.
For details, contact:
DK Publishing Special Markets
375 Hudson Street
New York, New York 10014
SpecialSales@dk.com

A catalog record for this book
is available from the Library of Congress

ISBN: 978-0-7566-2944-1 (Paperback)
ISBN: 978-0-7566-2945-8 (Hardcover)

Color reproduction by Colourscan, Singapore
Printed and bound in China by L Rex Printing Co., Ltd.

The publisher would like to thank the following for their kind
permission to reproduce their photographs:
a=above; b=below; c=center; l=left; r=right; t=top

Alamy Images: Available Light Photography 31b; David R. Frazier
Photolibrary, Inc. 8-9; Justin Kase 30b; Motoring Picture Library /
National Motor Museum 6t; Greg Randles 16-17; Robert Harding
Picture Library Ltd 10-11; Trevor Smithers ARPS 24-25t; Alan Stone
12-13; Mel Stuart 20t; vario images GmbH & Co.KG 4-5, 31t;
BAE Systems 2007 : 26tl, 26-27t; **Corbis**: George Hall 18-19t;
Mark M. Lawrence 29t; Gary I Rothstein / epa 28t; David Sailors
7t; Terraqua Images 22-23cb; Ronald Wittek / dpa 30t; **DK Images**:
Judith Miller / Wallis And Wallis 27bl (grey submarine); National
Maritime Museum, London 25br (trawler); **Ford Motor Company
Ltd**: 3b, 6bl, 7bl, 7br; **Getty Images**: Lori Adamski Peek 14t; Jim
Cummins 15; Ed Darack 22t; Richard Price 21t

All other images © Dorling Kindersley
For further information see: www.dkimages.com

Discover more at
www.dk.com

Contents

DK READERS

LEARNING
pre-level
1
TO READ

On the Move

DK Publishing

There are many ways to travel.

Cars go on the roads.
Vroom!
Off they go.

windshield

 cars

Trucks rumble along
the highway.
They carry heavy loads.

trailer

trucks

cab

A train moves fast along the railroad tracks.

engine

trains

t whizzes past.

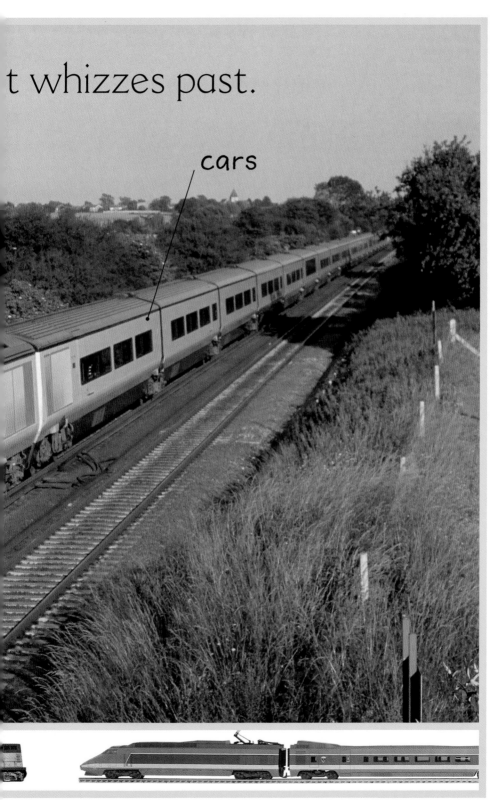

cars

Tractors drive on farms. They go up and down the fields.

cab

tractors

wheel

Bicycles go along
the paths.
The wheels go round
and round.

 bicycles

helmet

wheel

Buses go along the streets.
People get on and off.

buses

light

SCHOOL BUS

wing

Airplanes fly in the sky.
Zoom! Off they go.

 airplanes

engine

Hot-air balloons float
in the sky.
They go up, up, and away!

basket / \ burner

hot-air balloons

Helicopters whirr
through the air.
The blades spin around.

6684

helicopters

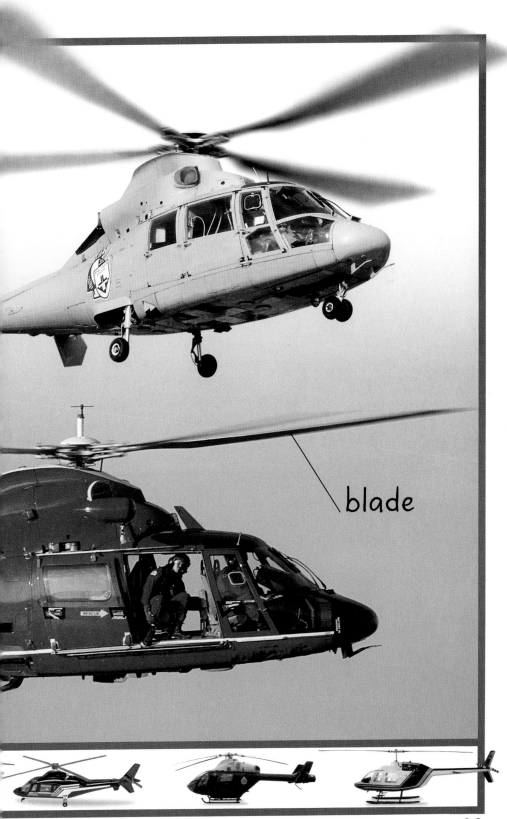

blade

Boats sail on the water.
They float over
the waves.

boats

flag

wave

 submarines

A submarine glides
through the sea.
It dives under the water.

The space shuttle zooms off into space.
Whoosh! Off it goes!

launchpad

space shuttles

Whoosh!

We can travel by air . . .

by road . . .

by train . . .

or by sea.

Which way do you like best?

Glossary

 **Bicycle** a vehicle with two wheels

 **Bus** a road vehicle that travels along a fixed route

 **Helicopter** an aircraft with spinning blades

 **Space shuttle** a flying vehicle that travels into space and back again

 **Tractor** a four-wheeled farm vehicle